Going Green

Making Cities Green

by Jeanette Leardi

Consultant: Frank Robbins, LEED AP
(Leadership in Energy and Environmental Design,
Accredited Professional)

BEARPORT
PUBLISHING

New York, New York

Credits

Cover and Title Page, © Thomas Jackson/Riser/Getty Images; 4-5, © Digital Vision Ltd./SuperStock; 6-7, © Anne Kitzman/Shutterstock; 8, © Gianni Muratore/Alamy; 9, © Lester Lefkowitz/Stone/Getty Images; 10-11, © Haxorjoe/Wikimedia; 11, © Martin Shields/Photo Researchers, Inc.; 13, © Peter Thompson/The New York Times/Redux Pictures; 15, © Bob Thomas/Popperfoto/Getty Images; 16-17, © Creatas/SuperStock; 17, © Khoroshunova Olga/Shutterstock; 18-19, © Lawrence Migdale/Photo Researchers, Inc.; 20-21, © Panoramic Images/Getty Images; 23, © Thomas Jackson/Riser/Getty Images; 24, © WENN/Newscom; 25L, © Mark Wilson/Newsmakers/Getty Images; 25R, © Jim West/Alamy; 26, Courtesy of Carbon Day/www.CarbonDay.com; 27, © Andre Jenny/Alamy; 28, © Dane Andrew/ZUMA Press; 29, © Ingram Publishing/Photolibrary; 30, © Morgan Lane Photography/iStockphoto.

Publisher: Kenn Goin
Editorial Director: Adam Siegel
Creative Director: Spencer Brinker
Photo Researcher: Picture Perfect Professionals, LLC

The Going Green series is
printed on recycled paper.

Library of Congress Cataloging-in-Publication Data

Leardi, Jeanette.
  Making cities green / by Jeanette Leardi.
     p. cm. — (Going green)
  Includes bibliographical references and index.
  ISBN-13: 978-1-59716-961-5 (library binding)
  ISBN-10: 1-59716-961-7 (library binding)
  1. Urban ecology (Sociology)—Juvenile literature. 2. Sustainable living—Juvenile literature. 3. Sustainable architecture—Juvenile literature. 4. Renewable energy resources—Juvenile literature. I. Title.

  HT241.L435 2010
  333.7209173'2—dc22
                                          2009019166

For more information, write to Bearport Publishing Company, Inc., 101 Fifth Avenue, Suite 6R, New York, New York 10003.
Printed in the United States of America.

10 9 8 7 6 5 4 3 2 1

Contents

Big Busy Cities

America's cities buzz with activity. Each day, millions of people travel around them in cars, buses, and subways—rushing to get to work, to shop, or to meet friends. Huge trucks travel the streets carrying goods to stores. Airplanes, boats, and trains bring in people from other places. Big cities are exciting. Yet they also cause big problems for our planet.

Many of these problems have to do with **fossil fuels**—namely, coal, oil, and gas. Cities use huge amounts of these fuels. They are burned at power plants to make electricity that a city uses to light its buildings and to run its computers, air conditioners, and many other machines. Fossil fuels also provide most of the **energy** needed to heat buildings and to run cars, buses, and trucks. Today we can't live without these fuels. At the same time, however, we can't go on using them as we have in the past.

Cities use huge amounts of energy because so many people live in them. In the United States today, 250 million people live in cities—that's about 82 percent of the U.S. population.

Reasons for Going Green

What problems come with using fossil fuels? One problem is that they are not **renewable**. Once people use up Earth's supply of coal, oil, and gas, these fuels can't be replaced.

Other problems occur when fossil fuels are burned. They give off poisonous chemicals that **pollute** the air, making it unhealthy for people to breathe in. They also release **greenhouse gases** such as **carbon dioxide**. Greenhouse gases trap heat from the sun, causing Earth's **atmosphere** to warm up. This effect, known as **global warming**, can kill many plants and animals that aren't able to live in warmer environments.

A coal-burning power plant near Cincinnati, Ohio

That's a lot of bad news. Fortunately, however, there's also good news. Some cities are finding big ways to cut down on their use of fossil fuels and to make other important changes that will help the environment. These cities are becoming known as "green" cities.

About 85 percent of the energy used in the United States comes from burning fossil fuels.

Clean, Green Energy

Instead of fossil fuels, a green city uses clean and renewable energy sources whenever possible. Clean energy sources do not release harmful chemicals or gases into the atmosphere. Renewable energy sources will never run out.

Wind is an energy source that is both clean and renewable. When wind turns the blades of a wind **turbine**, the blades spin a **generator** that produces electricity. Using wind turbines to produce electricity allows cities to reduce the amount of fossil fuels that they need. For example, the city of Houston, Texas, uses wind power to produce about one-fourth of its electric power.

Wind turbines on the roof of a building in London

One problem with using wind turbines in cities is that they take up a lot of space. People are solving this problem by placing small two-foot (61-cm) turbines on the roofs of buildings or placing larger wind turbines on land just outside of cities.

The sun is another clean and renewable energy source. **Solar panels** on the outside of buildings capture the power of the sun's rays. These panels contain **solar cells**, which change energy from sunlight into electrical power.

Solar panels on the roof of this building in New York City provide clean and renewable energy.

Green Buildings

More and more, green cities are using clean and renewable energy sources. Yet fossil fuels are still the main source of energy for lighting, heating, and cooling most city buildings. Finding ways to use less energy for these purposes helps **conserve** fossil fuels while at the same time making buildings—and the cities they are part of—greener.

One fairly simple way to save on electric lighting is to put in large windows and skylights that let in lots of sunlight. Modern **devices** can help, too. For example, light **sensors** automatically turn off the lights when there is no one in the room. Also, people can replace traditional lightbulbs with compact fluorescent lightbulbs (CFLs), which are four times more energy efficient and last longer. Even better are light-emitting diodes (LEDs). They use less energy than CFLs and last up to ten times longer.

Glass curtain walls, such as those in the New York Times *building, allow more natural light to shine through—reducing the building's use of electrical lighting.*

A traditional lightbulb

A compact fluorescent lightbulb

About 72 percent of all the electricity produced in the United States is used to run buildings.

Cooling Down

City buildings get hotter inside than buildings that are not in cities. Why? Sidewalks, streets, and rooftops **absorb** and hold more of the sun's heat than grassy or forested areas. The heat from these city surfaces rises and warms the air above. When the air outside gets hotter, the air inside buildings gets hotter, too. So people often turn up the air conditioning to stay cool. That means they use more electricity—and more fossil fuels. It also means that in order to become greener, cities have to find ways to keep their air temperatures down.

One way to cool a city down is to grow trees, grass, and other plants in parks, along streets, and even on rooftops. Trees provide shade from the sun, and grassy surfaces stay cooler than paved ones. Another way to lower the temperature is to pave sidewalks with light-colored materials that **reflect** sunlight rather than absorb it.

The pavement in a city on a hot summer day can heat up to 120–150°F (49–66°C). A city's air temperature at night can be up to 22°F (12°C) warmer than that of nearby areas outside the city.

A garden covers the roof of this McDonald's in Chicago.

Green Ways to Get Around

When people in a city aren't inside buildings, they're outside, going places. That's why city streets are often jammed with cars. Unfortunately, cars burn gas—a fossil fuel that pollutes the air and can contribute to global warming. Reducing the number of cars on streets can help a city to become green.

One way to cut down on the amount of cars in a city is to provide fast and convenient forms of public transportation, such as subways and buses. Some cities like Portland, Oregon, have light rail systems. The vehicles that make up a light rail system run on electricity. They usually travel on tracks that are set apart from the roads where cars travel in order to avoid traffic. Because a large number of people can ride together on a subway, bus, or light rail vehicle, these forms of transportation burn less fuel per person than cars.

A great way to get around a city without using any fuel at all is biking. Many cities provide special lanes and paths for bikes. They also provide outdoor racks where people can leave and lock their bikes.

Some cities have pedestrian malls, where no cars are allowed and where people can walk among stores and restaurants.

The energy-saving light rail system in Houston, Texas, runs on electricity and even allows riders with bicycles to board.

Recycling Trash

Using up fossil fuels and releasing greenhouse gases aren't the only problems that cities cause. Another problem is that cities create a huge amount of garbage. Where does it all go?

More than half of it is dumped into **landfills**. While some of the garbage in landfills breaks down and turns into soil, some does not. For example, glass never breaks down, and plastics and metals take thousands of years to break down. If people keep creating new landfills to hold all their trash, they will eventually cover the planet with garbage.

A bulldozer pushing garbage in a landfill

Many cities are reducing the amount of garbage placed in landfills by encouraging people to **recycle**. These cities provide people with special containers for metal, glass, paper, and plastic trash. Trucks take these materials to recycling centers. From there, the materials are sent to factories where they are turned into new metal, glass, paper, and plastic—which can then be made into useful items.

Each person in the United States throws away about four and a half pounds (2 kg) of trash every day. That's about 1,642 pounds (745 kg) per person per year.

Recycling containers

PLASTIC PAPER CANS

Recycling Water

In addition to creating a lot of garbage, cities create a lot of wastewater. Wastewater is water that has been used for purposes such as flushing toilets and washing. It's any water that goes down a drain.

Why is wastewater a problem? Water is renewable—we get more of it every time it rains. However, big cities sometimes use up more water than is replaced by rain. If too much water goes down drains, a city could have a shortage of drinking water.

A solution to the wastewater problem is recycling. Many cities have water treatment **plants** that clean used, dirty water. Some plants can even make wastewater clean enough to drink. Most plants, however, pipe the treated water to sprinklers that water grass and trees in parks so that drinking water doesn't have to be used for this purpose.

A water treatment plant in Oakland, California

In a water treatment plant, wastewater flows through screens that catch particles of dirt. Then the water is treated with chemicals that make it cleaner.

Growing Cities

Many people want to live in cities. They like living near their jobs, and they like living in places where there's a lot to do. For these reasons, the number of people living in cities—and the number of buildings in cities—usually keeps growing.

As a city grows, it often spreads outward. New buildings take over surrounding land that was once forest or farmland. This spreading of a city is called **urban sprawl**.

Urban sprawl is a tough problem. It can destroy the **habitats** where plants and animals live. It can also increase air pollution due to the increased number of cars people use to get around in a larger city. Fortunately, people in cities around the country are coming up with "green" solutions to reduce urban sprawl. One is to build bigger, taller buildings near a city's center, rather than having buildings spread outward. Another is for cities to set **growth boundaries**— borderlines beyond which no building is allowed. This approach protects a city's **greenbelt**—its surrounding area of parklands, wilderness, or farms.

Portland, Oregon's greenbelt is connected to the city by trails so that people can reach it on foot or by bike.

Greenbelts help reduce global warming because trees and other plants soak up carbon dioxide—a greenhouse gas.

Looking into the Future

Imagine flying over a city and looking down. The tops of most buildings are covered with green grass and trees. The blades of turbines on rooftops are spinning in the wind. Many buildings have shiny solar panels that sparkle in the sunlight.

Down below, the sidewalks are paved with light-colored material that stays cool, even on hot days. Trees line the streets, providing shade, and there are many parks. Only a few cars are on the streets. Many people are walking or riding bikes. Others are using buses or light rail systems to get around. In the center of the city, there is a pedestrian mall. Around the edges of the city is a greenbelt where people can bike, hike, and explore nature.

What city is this? It's a big city that has solved some big problems. It's a green city of the future.

Government organizations such as the U.S. Department of Energy and the Environmental Protection Agency enforce laws that make sure American cities are working to become greener.

Here is one artist's view of how a green city of the future might look.

Just the Facts

Cities across the United States are becoming green. Here are some of the ways they are doing it.

New York City

- In 2007, six electricity-generating turbines were placed underwater in New York City's East River in order to supply electricity to a nearby supermarket.

- The turbines look like underwater windmills. They generate electricity in the same way wind turbines do, but their blades are turned by the moving current of the river, rather than by wind.

- An advantage that underwater turbines have over wind turbines is that they don't take up space on land.

- One problem with underwater turbines, however, is that they can disturb or even kill fish and other sea creatures.

- Making green energy isn't always easy. The East River's current was so powerful that it damaged the turbines. However, New York City plans to install stronger turbines in order to produce enough electricity for 10,000 homes.

An underwater turbine being installed in New York City's East River

Washington, D.C.

- Washington, D.C., is one of the most bike-friendly cities in the country.

- The city has about 17 miles (27 km) of bike lanes and 50 miles (80 km) of bike paths.

- Throughout the downtown area, there are more than 400 bike racks that cyclists can use to lock up their bikes while they work or shop.

- All city buses have bike racks. Cyclists can hang their bikes on the racks while they're riding the bus.

- Cyclists can also take their bikes with them when they ride the city's subways.

Bike stations in Washington D.C., allow a person to rent a bike and then leave it off at another convenient location.

Chicago, Illinois

Chicago is getting ready for green cars. These vehicles are powered by electricity instead of fossil fuels. In April 2009, the city opened its first solar-powered electric vehicle charging station.

- Cars that run on electricity already exist. One of the problems with them, however, is that their batteries need to be recharged often. People who own these cars need charging stations the way other people need gas stations.

- At Chicago's charging station, the electricity for recharging cars comes from a set of solar panels that charge an underground battery during the daytime.

An electric car at Chicago's solar-powered charging station

Charlotte, North Carolina

ImaginOn, Charlotte's beautiful children's library and theater, was built in 2005, using lots of recycled materials.

- Stones from old monuments were used to make some of the building's walls.

- Sections of the floor were made from used rubber car tires.

- Plastic detergent bottles were crushed and then glued together to make colorful doors for the bathroom stalls.

- The concrete in the building was made with the ash that is produced when coal is burned.

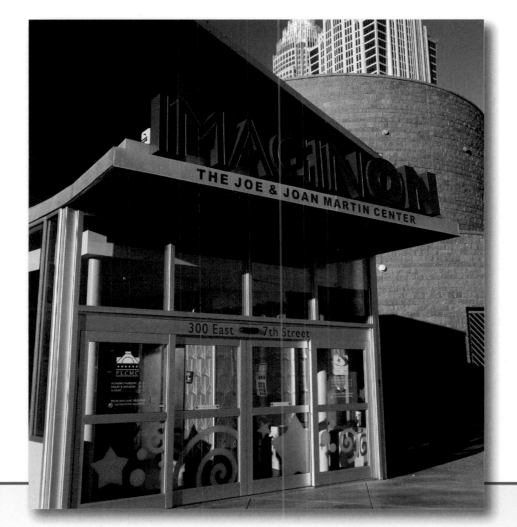

Oakland, California

In Oakland, California, electric buses run on batteries powered by hydrogen.

- In 2005, three hydrogen-powered buses began operating on the streets of Oakland.

- Hydrogen is a gas that releases nothing into the atmosphere but water vapor—invisible steam.

- Tanks on a bus's roof carry enough hydrogen for each bus to travel 300 to 350 miles (483 to 563 km).

- The buses glide quietly along downtown streets, making almost no sound at all.

- About 1,000 people ride on the buses each day.

- Oakland plans to put more hydrogen-powered buses on the streets.

Portland, Oregon

In 2008, Portland, Oregon, was named the "Greenest American City" by SustainLane, an environmental research organization. Here are some of the reasons:

- Portland was the first city in the United States to aim for lower greenhouse gas levels.

- Portland's growth boundary protects about 25 million acres (10,117,141 hectares) of farms and forests.

- Portland's public transportation system includes more than 90 bus lines.

- In 2008, people made more than 35 million trips on its light rail system.

Portland has 260 miles (418 km) of biking trails and lanes.

Index

Bibliography

http://trimet.org/pdfs/publications/factsheet.pdf

www.cleanfleetreport.com/clean-fleet-articles/california-hydrogen-highway-spans-800-miles/

www.eia.doe.gov/environment.html

www.sustainlane.com/us-city-rankings/cities/portland

www.thegreenguide.com/travel-transportation/what-makes-city-green

www2.actransit.org/environment/hyroad_main.wu?r=n

Read More

Bellamy, Rufus. *Clean Air.* North Mankato, MN: Smart Apple Media (2006).

Jefferis, David. *Green Power: Eco-Energy Without Pollution.* New York: Crabtree Publishing Company (2006).

Stern, Steven L. *Building Greenscrapers.* New York: Bearport (2010).

About the Author

Jeanette Leardi has written many educational books for children, as well as poems, articles, and essays for adults. She is the author of *The Great Pyramid: Egypt's Tomb for All Time* and *Southern Sea Otters: Fur-tastrophe Avoided.*